Keto Vegan Life Style

Healthy Eating For A Healthy Life With Delicious Plant-Based Recipes

Emma Wilson

TABLE OF CONTENTS

INTRODUCTION   9

BREAKFAST   13

VEGAN BREAKFAST MUFFINS   13
VEGAN BREAKFAST BISCUITS   14
AVOCADO MUG BREAD   15
VEGAN BREAKFAST SAUSAGES   16
QUICK BREAKFAST YOGURT   17
SPICED TOFU AND BROCCOLI SCRAMBLE   18
MEAT-FREE BREAKFAST CHILI   19
VEGAN SOUTHWESTERN BREAKFAST   20
NO-BREAD AVOCADO SANDWICH   21

LUNCH   23

KOREAN CUCUMBER SALAD   23
BEETS & SEEDS SALAD   24
AVOCADO MAYONNAISE   25
GOOSEBERRY SAUCE   26
NORI SALAD DRESSING   27
STUFFED PEPPERS   28
WALNUT & GARLIC SUMMER SQUASH   29
ONION FRITTERS   30
FRIED TOFU   31
COCONUT LEEK SOUP   32

DINNER   35

CABBAGE GARLIC SOUP   35
TOFU CHEESE NUGGETS & ZUCCHINI FRIES   36
AVOCADO SPRING ROLLS   38
CAULIFLOWER CURRY SOUP   40
ROASTED VEGETABLES WITH HERBS   42
CHEESECAKE CUPS   44

COCONUT APRICOTS SOUP   46

PUMPKIN COCONUT SOUP   47

TOMATOES COCONUT CREAM SOUP   48

PUMPKIN ALMOND SOUP   49

SNACKS   51

SWEET POTATO TOAST   51

LOW-CARB CLOVER ROLLS   52

KETO BREAD ROLLS   54

SEEDED BUNS   56

MOUTABELLE WITH KETO FLATBREAD   58

VEGETABLE LATKES SPIKED WITH CURRY   60

VEGAN CHEESE FONDUE   61

CHOCOLATE PEANUT BUTTER COOKIES   62

VEGGIE WRAPS WITH GLORIOUS TAHINI SAUCE   63

NEVER FEAR THIN BAGELS PIECES   64

VERY WHITE CHOCOLATE PEANUT BUTTER BITES   66

DESSERTS   69

WONDERFUL PEANUT BUTTER MOUSSE   69

THE NO-BAKE KETO CHEESE CAKE   70

RASPBERRY CHOCOLATE CUPS   72

AWESOME ROASTED ACORN SQUASH   73

EXUBERANT PUMPKIN FUDGE   74

LUCKY MEDITERRANEAN STYLE PASTA   76

UNIQUE SCRAMBLED TOFU   78

QUICK CREAMED COCONUT CURRY SPINACH   80

VINTAGE MOIST ALMOND CAKE   82

ICONIC BRAISED ENDIVES   84

CONCLUSION   87

INTRODUCTION

A keto vegan diet is a hybrid diet that combines ketogenic and vegan diets into one dietary style. In order to better understand this hybrid diet, you should first understand each separate diet so that you can better see how they come together to form one united diet.

The keto diet is one that relies on high-fat intake and low-carb intake with a moderate amount of protein. This diet is said to boost your ability to enter a state of ketosis, which means that instead of using carbohydrates or sugars for fuel, your body is burning fat. Many people eat the keto diet in an effort to lose weight, while others benefit from the lower sugar intake. This diet has become more popular in the past five years as people have realized how powerful it actually is and how it can improve their general sense of wellbeing.

The vegan diet is one that is focused on eating a plant-based diet. Individuals who eat the vegan way cut out all animal products to avoid the exploitation and suffering of animals, as well as to support the environment and reap the many benefits of this diet. Vegans primarily eat fruits and vegetables, legumes, nuts and seeds, and whole grains. They also eat meat alternatives and dairy alternatives that were made to be vegan-friendly, although some vegans prefer to leave these alternatives out of their diet altogether as some of the alternatives can be considered "junk food" or unhealthy to eat.

The keto vegan diet, then, is a low-carb, high-fat diet in order to meet the keto standards, and it excludes all animal products in order to meet the vegan standards. This might sound rather challenging, especially because many vegetables, fruits, and whole-grains are high in natural sugars; however, it is possible with proper planning.

In order to reach the goals of the keto diet, keto vegans aim to eat less than 50 grams of carbohydrates per day to ensure that they remain in a state of ketosis. The remaining portion of the diet is eaten of different fats, then, rather than carbohydrates. With a standard diet, these fats would be derived from high-fat animal products such as butter, whole-fat dairy products, and a variety of different meats. With a vegan diet, these fats are derived from plants such as avocados, coconut oil, and a variety of different nuts and seeds.

There are many different benefits associated with both the keto and vegan diet, although no noteworthy studies focus specifically on both of these diets being consumed together. However, the health benefits of both are said to be present when you eat this way, allowing you to gain access to a variety of different benefits from eating a keto vegan diet.

The vegan diet specifically has been linked to many different health benefits. Reduced risk of chronic health conditions ranging from autoimmune disorders and type 2 diabetes to heart disease and a variety of different cancers are all benefits of veganism. As well, vegans tend to weigh less, clocking in much closer to healthier weight levels than non-vegans.

In addition to these significant benefits, more "average" day-to-day benefits have been reported from the vegan diet, as well. People who eat it report having more energy, feeling mentally clearer, and having fewer issues with mood swings and other emotional-related considerations. As well, vegans tend to have improved immunity to various common ailments that people may suffer from, including allergies and the common cold.

Keto has similar benefits to veganism. It is said to improve your ability to achieve and maintain a healthy weight while also being able to control and manage your blood glucose levels effectively. As well, the keto diet can significantly reduce heart disease risk factors both in people who are at risk of contracting heart disease or who have already developed it.

BREAKFAST

Vegan Breakfast Muffins

Preparation Time: 5 minutes - Cooking Time: 3 minutes - Servings: 3

Ingredients:

- 2 tbsp. Almond Flour
- ½ tsp Baking Powder
- ½ tsp Salt
- 2 tbsp. Ground Flax Seeds
- ¼ cup Coconut Milk
- 3 tbsp. Avocado Oil

Directions:

1. Whisk together almond flour, ground flax, baking powder, and salt in a bowl.
2. Stir in coconut milk
3. Heat avocado oil in a non-stick pan.
4. Ladle in the batter and cook for 2-3 minutes per side.

Nutrition: Calories 194 / Carbohydrates 2 g / Fats 21 g / Protein 1 g

Vegan Breakfast Biscuits

Preparation Time: 10 minutes - Cooking Time: 10 min. - Servings: 6

Ingredients:

- 1.5 cups Almond Flour
- 1 tbsp. Baking Powder
- ¼ tsp Salt
- ½ tsp Onion Powder
- ½ cup Coconut Milk
- ¼ cup Nutritional Yeast
- 2 tbsp. Ground Flax Seeds
- ¼ cup Olive Oil

Directions:

1. Preheat oven to 450°F.
2. Whisk together all ingredients in a bowl.
3. Divide the batter into a pre-greased muffin tin.
4. Bake for 10 minutes.

Nutrition: Calories 306 / Carbohydrates 10 g / Fats 28 g / Protein 7 g

Avocado Mug Bread

Preparation Time: 2 minutes - Cooking Time: 2 minutes - Servings: 1

Ingredients:

- ¼ cup Almond Flour
- ½ tsp Baking Powder
- ¼ tsp Salt
- ¼ cup Mashed Avocados
- 1 tbsp. Coconut Oil

Directions:

1. Mix all ingredients in a microwave-safe mug.
2. Microwave for 90 seconds.
3. Cool for 2 minutes.

Nutrition: Calories 317 / Carbohydrates 9 g / Fats 30 g / Protein 6 g

Vegan Breakfast Sausages

Preparation Time: 15 minutes - Cooking Time: 12 min. - Servings: 4

Ingredients:
- 200 grams Portobella Mushrooms
- 150 grams Walnuts
- 1 tbsp. Tomato Paste
- 75 grams Panko
- 1 tsp Paprika
- 1 tsp Dried Sage
- 1 tsp Salt
- ½ tsp Black Pepper

Directions:
1. Blend all ingredients in a food processor.
2. Divide mixture into serving-sized portions and shape into sausages.
3. Bake for 12 minutes at 375°F.

Nutrition: Calories 271 / Carbohydrates 9 g / Fats 25 g / Protein 7 g

Quick Breakfast Yogurt

Preparation Time: 2 minutes - Cooking Time: 8 minutes - Servings: 6

Ingredients:

- 4 cups Full-Fat Coconut Milk
- 2 tbsp. Coconut Milk Powder
- 100 grams Strawberries, for serving

Directions:

1. Whisk together coconut milk and milk powder in a microwave safe bowl.
2. Heat on high for 8-9 minutes.
3. Top with fresh strawberries and choice of sweetener to serve.

Nutrition: Calories 186 / Carbohydrates 10 g / Fats 38 g / Protein 4 g

Spiced Tofu and Broccoli Scramble

Preparation Time: 5 minutes - Cooking Time: 3 minutes - Servings: 3

Ingredients:

- 400 grams Firm Tofu, drained and pressed
- 1 tbsp. Tamari
- 1 tbsp. Garlic Powder
- 2 tsp Paprika Powder
- 2 tsp Turmeric Powder
- 150 grams Broccoli, rough-chopped
- 2 tbsp. Olive Oil

Directions:

1. Crumble the tofu in a bowl with the garlic powder, paprika, turmeric, and nutritional yeast.
2. Heat olive oil in a pan.
3. Sautee broccoli for a minute.
4. Stir in spiced tofu. Cook for 1-2 minutes.
5. Season with tamari. Serve hot.

Nutrition: Calories 231 / Carbohydrates 7 g / Fats 17 g / Protein 16 g

Meat-Free Breakfast Chili

Preparation Time: 10 minutes - Cooking Time: 20 min. - Servings: 4

Ingredients:

- 400 grams Textured-Vegetable Protein
- ¼ cup Red Kidney Beans
- ½ cup Canned Diced Tomatoes
- 1 Large Bell Pepper, diced
- 1 Large White Onion, diced
- 1 tsp Cumin Powder
- 1 tsp Chili Powder
- 1 tsp Paprika - 2 cups Water
- 1 tsp Garlic Powder
- ½ tsp Dried Oregano

Directions:

1. Combine all ingredients in a pot.
2. Simmer for 20 minutes.
3. Serve with your favorite bread or some slices of fresh avocado.

Nutrition: Calories 174 / Carbohydrates 9 g / Fats 9 g / Protein 18 g

Vegan Southwestern Breakfast

Preparation Time: 10 minutes - Cooking Time: 5 min. - Servings: 6

Ingredients:

- 1 small White Onion, diced
- 1 Bell Pepper, diced
- 150 grams Mushrooms, sliced
- 400 grams Firm Tofu, crumbled
- 1 tsp Turmeric Powder - 1 tbsp. Garlic Powder
- 2 tbsp. Nutritional Yeast
- ¼ cup Chopped Green Onions
- 2 cups Fresh Spinach - 1 cup Cherry Tomatoes
- 2 cups Baked Beans - 2 tbsp. Olive Oil

Directions:

1. Sautee onions, bell peppers, and mushrooms until onions are translucent. Add in the tofu.
2. Stir in the turmeric, garlic powder, and nutritional yeast.
3. Add green onions and spinach. Sautee for 1-2 minutes.
4. Serve with baked beans and cherry tomatoes.

Nutrition: Calories 174 /Carbohydrates 10 g / Fats 10 g / Protein 13 g

No-Bread Avocado Sandwich

Preparation Time: 10 minutes - Cooking Time: 0 min. - Servings: 2

Ingredients:

- 2 oz. little gem lettuce, 2 leaves extracted
- ½ oz. vegan butter
- 1 oz. sliced vegan cheese
- 1 avocado, pitted, peeled, and sliced
- 1 large red tomato, sliced
- Chopped fresh parsley to garnish

Directions:

1. Rinse and pat dry the lettuce leave.
2. Arrange on a flat plate (with inner side facing you) to serve as the base of the sandwich.
3. Spread some butter on each leaf, top with the cheese, avocado, and tomato.
4. Garnish with some parsley and serve the sandwich immediately.

Nutrition: Calories: 143 / Total Fat: 12.7 g / Saturated Fat: 4.3 g Total Carbs: 6 g / Dietary Fiber: 4 g / Sugar: 1 g / Protein: 4 g Sodium: 87 mg

LUNCH

Korean Cucumber Salad

Preparation Time: 10 min. - Cooking Time: 5 min. - Servings: 4

Ingredients

- 4 cucumbers, sliced
- 1 onion, chopped in semi circles
- 2-3 sprigs spring onions, finely chopped
- 2-3 garlic cloves, crushed
- 3 tsp sesame seeds, toasted
- 2 tsp red pepper flakes
- 3 Tbsp. soy sauce - 3 tsp sesame oil
- 2 tsp keto friendly sweetener you are using

Directions

1. Combine all ingredients.
2. Stir well and serve.

Nutrition: Carbs: 11 g / Fat: 5 g / Protein: 3 g / Calories: 112

Beets & Seeds Salad

Preparation Time: 15 min. - Cooking Time: 1 min. - Servings: 2

Ingredients

- 1 beet, boiled, grated
- 1 Tbsp. flaxseeds
- 1 Tbsp. toasted sunflower seeds
- 1 Tbsp. toasted walnuts, chopped
- 3 prunes, chopped
- For the dressing:
- 1 tsp tahini
- 1 garlic clove, minced
- 2 Tbsp. olive oil
- Salt to taste

Directions

1. Prepare the dressing by combining all dressing ingredients.
2. Combine all salad ingredients in a bowl and mix well.
3. Dress the salad and serve.

Nutrition: Carbs: 12 g / Fat: 21 g / Protein: 6.6 g / Calories: 251

Avocado Mayonnaise

Preparation Time: 10 min. - Cooking Time: 1 min. - Servings: 4

Ingredients

- 1 avocado
- 3 Tbsp. olive oil
- ½ jalapeño, chopped
- 3 garlic cloves, chopped
- ½ lemon, juiced
- 6-10 parsley sprigs, chopped
- Salt to taste

Directions

1. Combine all ingredients in a blender and pulse on high until smooth.
2. Keep refrigerated.

Nutrition: Carbs: 0 g / Fat: 11 g / Protein: 0 g / Calories: 90

Gooseberry Sauce

Preparation Time: 30 min.

Cooking Time: 5 min.

Servings: 4

Ingredients

- 5 cups gooseberries, rinsed, topped and tailed
- 5 garlic cloves, crushed
- 1 cup fresh dill, rinsed, stems removed
- Salt to taste

Directions

1. Combine gooseberries and dill in a blender and pulse until smooth.
2. Add garlic and salt.
3. Let stand for 30 minutes, covered.

Nutrition: Carbs: 8 g / Fat: 2 g / Protein: 1 g / Calories: 35

Nori Salad Dressing

Preparation Time: 5 min.

Cooking Time: 0 min.

Servings: 6

Ingredients

- 2 toasted nori sheets
- 2 Tbsp. sesame oil
- ¾ cup rice wine vinegar
- 1 Tbsp. orange zest
- ½ tsp sea salt

Directions

1. Break the toasted nori into small pieces.
2. Add all ingredients in a blender and pulse on high.
3. Serve the nori dressing over roasted vegetables.
4. Keep refrigerated.

Nutrition: Carbs: 0.5 g / Fat: 1.5 g / Protein: 0.3 g / Calories: 18

Stuffed Peppers

Preparation Time: 15 min. - Cooking Time: 30 min. - Servings: 2

Ingredients

- 1 large bell pepper, halved, deseeded
- 1 medium eggplant, rinsed, cubed
- 1 tomato, peeled, cubed - 1 onion, chopped
- 1 carrot, grated - 2 sprigs basil
- 1 garlic clove, crushed - 2 Tbsp. olive oil
- Salt and pepper to taste

Directions

1. Add half the onion to a preheated pan with olive oil. Season with salt and pepper. Add eggplant and fry until golden.
2. In a stewpot sauté the remaining onion with carrots.
3. Season with salt and pepper.
4. Add tomatoes and garlic to the carrots.
5. Cook for 10 minutes, covered, over medium heat.
6. Fill the pepper halves with eggplant and onions.
7. Place the stuffed peppers into the stewpot.
8. Stew for 15 minutes until the pepper is soft.

Nutrition: Carbs: 13 g / Fat: 7.7 g / Protein: 5 g / Calories: 199

Walnut & Garlic Summer Squash

Preparation Time: 15 min. - Cooking Time: 10 min. - Servings: 4

Ingredients

- 2 lbs. green summer squash, rinsed, cubed
- ½ cup walnuts, crushed
- 3 garlic cloves, crushed
- 10 sprigs parsley, minced
- 2 Tbsp. + 1 Tbsp. vegetable oil

Directions

1. In a preheated pan with oil, add cubed squash and cook over high heat until soft.
2. In a bowl, combine minced parsley, garlic, walnuts and 1 Tbsp. oil. Mix well.
3. Add the walnut mixture to the pan and mix well.
4. Turn the heat off.
5. Serve warm or cooled to your liking.

Nutrition: Carbs: 10 g / Fat: 20 g / Protein: 5.3 g / Calories: 239

Onion Fritters

Preparation Time: 5 min. - Cooking Time: 20 min. - Servings: 4

Ingredients

- 3 large onions, peeled
- 4 leeks
- 6 Tbsp. Keto friendly flour (almond/coconut)
- ¼ tsp fish seasoning
- Salt and pepper to taste

Directions

1. Chop the onions and leeks and add to the food processor.
2. Pulse until smooth.
3. To the pureed onions add flour and seasonings.
4. In a preheated pan with oil, spoon out the fritters and fry until golden on each side over high heat.

Nutrition: Carbs: 13 g / Fat: 11 g / Protein: 5 g / Calories: 186

Fried Tofu

Preparation Time: 5 min. - Cooking Time: 10 min. - Servings: 4

Ingredients

- 1 lb. tofu, cubed - 2 tomatoes, chopped
- 1 chili pepper, chopped - ½ cup onion, chopped
- 2 garlic cloves, minced - 1 Tbsp. olive oil
- 1 Tbsp. lime juice - 1 tsp ground chili
- ½ tsp cumin - ½ tsp oregano - Salt to taste

Directions

1. In a preheated pan with olive oil pan add fresh chili pepper, onions, garlic and fry stirring for 4 minutes.
2. Season with ground chili, cumin, oregano, and salt.
3. Cook, stirring, 30 seconds.
4. Add tofu to the pan and lower the heat.
5. Cook, stirring, for 5 minutes.
6. Right before serving, top with lime juice.
7. Serve with fresh tomatoes.

Nutrition: Carbs: 2.5 g / Fat: 5.7 g / Protein: 5 g / Calories: 76

Coconut Leek Soup

Preparation Time: 5 min. - Cooking Time: 30 min. - Servings: 4

Ingredients

- 1 leek, circled - 1 carrot, sliced
- 3 celery stalks, sliced - ½ lemon, juiced
- 1½ cup coconut milk - 1 tsp curry
- 3 Tbsp. grated ginger root - ½ tsp salt
- 2 Tbsp. olive oil - 2 cups water

Directions

1. Add the leeks, carrots, and celery to a pot with olive oil and some water. Let stew until the vegetables are soft.
2. Add 1½ cup water and 1½ cup coconut milk and bring to boil.
3. Cook for 2 minutes on low.
4. Add lemon juice, ginger, curry, and salt and cook on low for 2 minutes.

Nutrition: Carbs: 11 g / Fat: 9.6 g / Protein: 3.6 g / Calories: 142

DINNER

Cabbage Garlic Soup

Preparation Time: 10 min. - Cooking Time: 35 min. - Servings: 4

Ingredients:

- 10 cloves of garlic - 1 cabbage
- 5 onions - 2 carrots
- 7 tbsp. Olive oil - half chili pepper
- salt and pepper - chives, chopped

Directions:

1. Chop the garlic, onions and cabbage, heat the oil in a frying pan or wok and fry the vegetables for 10 minutes stirring all the time.
2. Peel and cut the carrots into cubes and fry for 5 minutes with the other vegetables.
3. Place all the vegetables to a saucepan and boil for 20 min.
4. Sprinkle with the chopped fresh chives and serve.

Nutrition: Calories: 127 / Total fat: 19 oz. / Total carbohydrates: 4 oz. Protein: 8 oz.

Tofu Cheese Nuggets & Zucchini Fries

Preparation Time: 5 minutes

Cooking Time: 18 min.

Servings: 2

Ingredients:

Tofu Cheese Nuggets:

- 1 (12 oz. pack) extra firm tofu, drained, cubed
- ½ cup smoked chipotle cream cheese
- ½ cup almond flour
- 2 tbsp. water

Zucchini Fries:

- 2 tsp. red chili flakes
- ½ cup almond flour
- ¼ cup olive oil
- 1 large zucchini, skinned

Directions:

1. Preheat the oven to 400°F and line a baking tray with parchment paper.

2. Put the cream cheese, ½ cup almond flour, and water into a large bowl and mix thoroughly until all the ingredients are combined.

3. Add the tofu cubes to the bowl and coat all the cubes evenly.

4. Transfer the coated tofu cubes onto one half of the baking tray and set it aside.

5. Put the chili flakes and almond flour into a large bowl and mix until all ingredients are combined.

6. Pour the olive oil into a medium-sized bowl and dip each zucchini stick into the oil. Make sure to cover all fries evenly.

7. Put the zucchini fries in the bowl with the almond flour mixture and gently stir the fries around until they are all evenly covered.

8. Transfer the zucchini fries onto the baking tray with the tofu nuggets and spread them out evenly. If the nuggets and fries don't fit on the baking tray together, bake them in two batches.

9. Put the baking tray into the oven and bake the nuggets and fries for about 18 minutes, or until golden-brown and crispy.

10. Take the baking tray out of the oven and let the dish cool down for about a minute.

11. Serve and enjoy with a light salad of greens as a side dish.

Nutrition:

Calories 813.5 / Carbohydrates 7 g / Fats 72.1 g / Protein 30.35 g

Avocado Spring Rolls

Preparation Time: 20 minutes - Cooking Time: 1 min. - Servings: 4

Ingredients:

- 2 medium Hass avocados, peeled, pitted, sliced
- 1-inch piece ginger, grated
- 1 garlic clove, minced
- Juice of ½ lemon
- ½ cup cabbage, shredded
- ¼ cup carrots, julienned or matchsticks
- 4-6 coconut wraps
- 2 tbsp. olive oil

Spicy Almond Sauce:

- ½ cup almond butter
- 2 tsp. low-sodium soy sauce
- ½ tsp. rice vinegar
- Juice of ½ lemon
- ½ tsp. chili garlic paste
- 1 tbsp. low-carb maple syrup
- 2 tsp. sesame oil

Directions:

1. In a small bowl, gently toss together the sliced avocado, ginger, garlic, lemon juice, cabbage, and julienned carrots.

2. Put a coconut wrap on a flat and dry surface. Place about ¼ of the avocado mixture in the center of the wrap.

3. Fold the wrap about ½ inch inward on two parallel sides and roll the wrap up until the mixture is covered.

4. Repeat with the remaining 3-5 wraps until all of the avocado mixture is used.

5. Put a skillet over medium-high heat and warm the olive oil until shimmering.

6. Add the spring rolls to the skillet and brown them, about 30 seconds on each side.

7. Prepare the sauce by putting all the sauce ingredients into a medium-sized bowl and stir thoroughly. Add one or more tablespoon of warm water, if necessary, to achieve the desired consistency.

8. Serve the spring rolls warm with the spicy almond sauce as a dip and enjoy!

Nutrition:

Calories 503 / Carbohydrates 11 g / Fats 45 g / Protein 10 g

Cauliflower Curry Soup

Preparation Time: 5 minutes - Cooking Time: 40 min. - Servings: 4

Ingredients:
- 1 large cauliflower, chopped
- 4 tbsp. olive oil
- ½ red onion, finely chopped
- 4 garlic cloves, minced
- 1 tbsp. yellow curry paste
- 1-inch piece ginger, grated
- 1 (12 oz. pack) extra firm tofu, drained, scrambled
- 1 tsp. chili flakes
- Juice of 1 medium lime
- 4 cups vegetable broth
- 1 tbsp. sesame oil
- 1 tsp. low-sodium soy sauce
- 1 cup full-fat coconut milk

Directions:

1. Preheat the oven to 400°F and line a baking tray with parchment paper.

2. Put the cauliflower florets on the baking tray and drizzle 2 tablespoons of olive oil over them, covering them evenly.

3. Put the baking tray into the oven and bake for about 25-30 minutes, until the florets are golden brown.

4. Put a large pot over medium heat and add the remaining 2 tablespoons of olive oil.

5. Take the baking tray out of the oven and set it aside for a few minutes to let the cauliflower florets cool down.

6. Add the onion and garlic to the pot and fry for about a minute, stirring occasionally.

7. Add the curry paste to the pot along with the ginger, scrambled tofu, and chili flakes. Stir for another minute.

8. Put the baked cauliflower florets into a blender or food processor, along with the vegetable broth, sesame oil, soy sauce, and coconut milk.

9. Blend these ingredients until smooth, then transfer the mixture into the pot.

10. Incorporate all the ingredients, stirring occasionally until the contents of the pot start to cook. Once the soup reaches the boiling point, bring the heat down to a simmer.

11. Cover the pot and let the soup simmer for about 10 minutes, then take the pot off the heat and set it aside to cool for a few minutes.

12. Enjoy!

Nutrition:

Calories 390.5 g / Carbohydrates 6 g / Fats 34.2 g / Protein 12.25 g

Roasted Vegetables with Herbs

Preparation Time: 10 minutes - Cooking Time: 40 min. - Servings: 4

Ingredients:

- 1 red bell pepper, deveined and sliced
- 1 green bell pepper, deveined and sliced
- 1 orange bell pepper, deveined and sliced
- ½ head of cauliflower, broken into large florets
- 2 zucchinis, cut into thick slices
- 2 medium-sized leeks, quartered
- 4 garlic cloves, halved
- 2 thyme sprigs, chopped
- 1 teaspoon dried sage, crushed
- 4 tablespoons olive oil
- 4 tablespoons tomato puree
- 1 teaspoon mixed whole peppercorns
- Sea salt and cayenne pepper, to taste

Directions:

1. Preheat your oven to 425°F.

2. Sprits a rimmed baking sheet with a nonstick cooking spray.

3. Toss all of the above vegetables with the seasonings, oil and apple cider vinegar.

4. Roast about 40 minutes.

5. Flip the vegetables halfway through the cooking time.

6. Bon appétit!

Nutrition:

Calories 321 / Carbohydrates 4 g / Fats 27.9 g / Protein 10.7 g

Cheesecake Cups

Preparation Time: 10 minutes - Cooking Time: 4 min. - Servings: 12

Ingredients:

Crust:

- ½ cup pumpkin seeds, raw
- 6 tbsp. shredded coconut, unsweetened
- 3 tbsp. coconut oil
- 2 tbsp. organic soy protein, vanilla flavor
- ½ tsp. stevia powder
- Pinch of salt

Filling:

- 6 tbsp. coconut oil
- 6 tbsp. almond butter
- 6 tbsp. coconut cream
- 2 tbsp. lemon juice
- 2 tbsp. organic soy protein, vanilla flavor
- Pinch of salt
- ¼ tsp. xanthan gum
- ¼ tsp. stevia powder

Directions:

1. Line a cupcake tin with 6 cupcake liners. Heat a small frying pan over medium-high heat.

2. Toast the pumpkin seeds in the frying pan, stirring occasionally for about 4 minutes. Add the shredded coconut and stir thoroughly to toast everything evenly.

3. Take the frying pan off the heat and allow the ingredients to cool down before transferring them into a food processor or blender. Pulse the pumpkin seeds and shredded coconut into small crumbs.

4. Transfer the crumbs to a medium-sized bowl and add the remaining crust ingredients.

5. Combine all ingredients into a thick dough and divide this mixture into six equal-sized balls.

6. Put one ball into each of the cupcake liners, pressing and flattening the balls into a crust at the bottom of each cupcake liner. Transfer the tin into the freezer and prepare the filling.

7. Heat a medium-sized saucepan over medium heat and add the coconut oil. Remove the saucepan from the heat once the coconut oil has melted.

8. Put the melted coconut oil, almond butter, coconut cream, lemon juice, organic soy protein, and a pinch of salt to the (uncleaned) food processor or blender. Process these ingredients until well combined with a smooth and creamy texture.

9. Add the optional xanthan gum and stevia. Xanthan gum will help thicken the cheesecake fat bombs, while the stevia will add a sweeter flavor. Use slightly more or less stevia to taste.

10. Take the cupcake tin out of the freezer and top all crusts with filling. Make sure to divide the filling equally among the 6 cups with a tablespoon.

11. Transfer the tin back into the fridge until the cups are firm.

12. Serve the cheesecake cups at room temperature and enjoy!

Nutrition:

Calories 217 / Carbohydrates 3 g / Fats 21.2 g / Protein 4.2 g

Coconut Apricots Soup

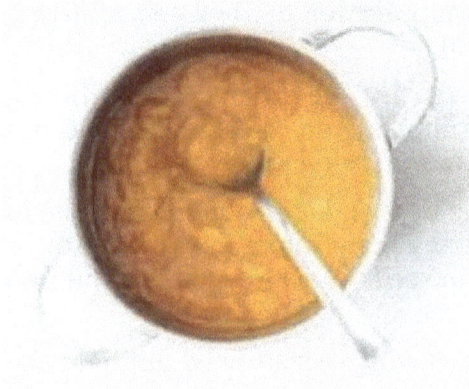

Preparation Time: 10 min. - Cooking Time: 25 min. - Servings: 4

Ingredients:

- 7 tbsp. coconut, shredded
- 3 cups coconut milk
- 15 oz. apricots, cubed
- 1 cup water
- 3 tbsp. erythritol
- a piece of ginger, not bigger than a hazelnut

Directions:

1. Cut the ginger into small pieces and send into a pan with a cup of water and boil for 10 minutes.
2. Pour the coconut milk and boil for 5 minutes, and then add the shredded coconut, apricots and erythritol.
3. Boil the coconut soup for 10 minutes and then serve.

Nutrition: Calories: 129 / Total fat: 37 oz. / Total carbohydrates: 7 oz. Protein: 15 oz.

Pumpkin Coconut Soup

Preparation Time: 10 min. - Cooking Time: 30 min. - Servings: 4

Ingredients:

- 2 lb. pumpkin
- 3 cups of water
- 1 cup coconut milk
- 2 tbsp. coconut cream
- 1 tbsp. Erythritol - salt

Directions:

1. Peel the pumpkin, remove the skin and seeds, and then cut into cubes and put into a pan.
2. Pour the water and boil the pumpkin for 15 minutes until soft and tender.
3. Blend the pumpkin using a blender or food processor until the homogenous mass.
4. Pour the water and coconut milk, smashed pumpkin, coconut cream, erythritol and salt to a saucepan and then cook for 15 minutes and serve!

Nutrition: Calories: 149 / Total fat: 39 oz. / Total carbohydrates: 4 oz. Protein: 12 oz.

Tomatoes Coconut Cream Soup

Preparation Time: 10 min. - Cooking Time: 25 min. - Servings: 4

Ingredients:

- 4 tomatoes
- 8 tbsp. coconut cream
- 8 garlic cloves
- 2 onions
- 2 tbsp. garlic powder
- 4 tbsp. sesame seeds oil
- salt and pepper

Directions:

1. Cut the tomatoes into cubes and fry them with the coconut cream for 5 minutes stirring all the time.
2. Add the tomatoes, garlic powder, some salt and ground pepper to a saucepan and boil for 10 minutes.
3. Chop the onions with garlic and then combine with the soup and boil for 10 minutes to serve.

Nutrition: Calories: 209 / Total fat: 26 oz. /Total carbohydrates: 5 oz. Protein: 11 oz.

Pumpkin Almond Soup

Preparation Time: 10 min. - Cooking Time: 50 min. - Servings: 4

Ingredients:

- 5 oz. pumpkin, cubed - 1 onion, chopped
- 7 tbsp. almond flour - 2 celery stalks, chopped
- 5 cups of vegetable broth - 7 tbsp. Olive oil
- 5 fresh basil leaves - Herbes de Provence
- salt and pepper

Directions:

1. Heat the water in a saucepan and boil the pumpkin for 20 minutes until soft.
2. Heat the oil in a frying pan or wok and fry the onions for about 5 minutes until clear.
3. Spoon the almond flour and mix well and then add the celery and fry for 10 min.
4. Add all the vegetables and vegetable broth to a saucepan with the pumpkin and boil for 15 min.
5. Add the basil and spices and serve.

Nutrition: Calories: 230 / Total fat: 21 oz. / Total carbohydrates: 5 oz. Proteins: 8 oz.

SNACKS

Sweet Potato Toast

Preparation Time: 3 minutes - Cooking Time: 20 min. - Servings: 4

Ingredients:

- 1 Ripe avocado
- 1 Large sweet potato
- Pepper and salt
- ½ cup Roughly-chopped pistachios
- 3 tbsp. Olive oil
- Crushed red pepper flakes

Directions:

1. Warm up the oven to 400°F.
2. Prepare a baking sheet with aluminum foil.
3. Slice the potato into 1/4-inch rounds.
4. Arrange on the baking sheet and toss it with the oil, salt, and pepper.
5. Bake for 20 minutes and garnish with the avocado and pistachios.
6. Add a few pepper flakes.

Nutrition: Calories 132 / Carbohydrates 7 g / Fats 11 g / Protein 2 g

Low-carb clover rolls

Preparation Time: 10 minutes

Cooking Time: 20 min.

Servings: 8

Ingredients:

- I/3 cup coconut flour
- 1 1/2 cup mozzarella cheese, shredded
- 1 1/2 teaspoon baking powder
- 1/4 cup parmesan cheese, grated
- 2 ounces cream cheese
- 2 eggs, large

Directions:

1. Preheat your oven to 350°F.

2. Put your almond flour and baking powder in a clean bowl and mix.

3. Using another bowl, put your Mozzarella and cream cheese and microwave for a minute.

4. Stir it well after it melts.

5. Add eggs to the cheese and stir.

6. Add the egg-cheese mix to the bowl with dry ingredients and mix thoroughly.

7. Wet your hands and knead dough into a sticky ball.

8. Put the dough ball on the parchment paper and slice into fourths.

9. Slice each fourth or quarter into 6 smaller portions.

10. Roll each small portion into balls.

11. Roll the balls into the parmesan cheese light for them to coat it.

12. Grease your muffin pan and place 3 dough balls in each cup of the pan.

13. Bake it for 20 minutes at 350°F.

Nutrition: Calories 283 / Carbohydrates 6 g / Fats 21 g / Protein 16 g

Keto bread rolls

Preparation Time: 10 minutes

Cooking Time: 20 min.

Servings: 8

Ingredients:

- 1 1/3 cups almond flour
- 1 1/2 cups shredded mozzarella cheese, part skim
- 2 oz. cream cheese, full fat
- 1 1/2 tablespoon baking powder, aluminum free
- 2 tablespoons coconut flour
- 3 eggs

Directions:

1. Preheat your oven to 350°F

2. In a clean bowl, put almond flour, coconut flour and baking powder. Mix well and set it aside.

3. Using a microwave-safe bowl, put the cream cheese and mozzarella in it and microwave for 30 seconds.

4. Remove the bowl, stir and microwave again for 30 seconds. This should go on until the cheese has entirely melted.

5. Using a food processor add the cheese, the eggs and flour mix. Process at high speed for uniformity of the dough. (It is normally sticky.)

6. Knead the dough into a dough ball and separate it into 8 equal pieces. Slightly wet your hands with oil for this step.

7. Roll each piece with your palms to form a ball and place each ball on the baking sheet. (should be 2 inches apart)

8. In a bowl, add the remaining egg and whisk. Brush the egg wash on the rolls.

9. Bake for 20 minutes or until they are golden brown.

Nutrition: Calories 216 / Carbohydrates 6 g / Fats 16 g / Protein 11 g

Seeded Buns

Preparation Time: 10 minutes

Cooking Time: 35 min.

Servings: 6

Ingredients:

- 1 cup almond flour
- 2 tsp. baking powder
- 3 egg whites
- 1.25 cup hot water
- 2 tbsp. sesame seeds
- 5 tbsp. psyllium husk powder
- 1 tsp. salt
- 2 tsp. apple cider vinegar
- medium saucepan
- standard sized flat sheet

Directions:

1. Warm the water in a saucepan until it starts to bubble. Transfer to a glass dish.

2. In the meantime, prepare a flat sheet with a layer of baking lining and set to the side.

3. Blend the water with the almond flour, baking powder, psyllium husk, salt, and apple cider vinegar until it becomes a thick consistency.

4. Section into 6 equal portions and form mounds.

5. Apply pressure to flatten the mounds to approximately 1 inch thick.

6. Arrange on the prepped flat sheet and glaze with the melted butter.

7. Dust with the sesame seeds and heat for approximately 35 minutes.

8. Serve immediately and enjoy!

Nutrition: Calories 73 / Carbohydrates 7 g / Fats 3 g / Protein 3 g

Moutabelle with Keto Flatbread

Preparation Time: 20 minutes - Cooking Time: 20 min.- Servings: 6

Ingredients:

For the Moutabelle

- 500 grams Eggplant
- 75 grams White Onion
- 10 grams Flat Parsley
- 2 tbsp. tahini paste
- 2 tbsp. Lemon Juice
- ¼ cup Olive Oil
- Salt, to taste
- Pepper, to taste

For the Flatbread:

- ½ cup Almond Flour
- 2 tbsp. Psyllium Husk
- ¼ tsp Baking Soda
- pinch of Salt
- 1 tbsp. Olive Oil
- 1 cup Lukewarm Water

Directions:

Prepare the Flatbread:

1. Whisk together the almond flour, psyllium husk, baking soda, and salt in a bowl.

2. Add in the water and olive oil.

3. Knead until everything comes together into a smooth dough.

4. Leave to rest for about 15 minutes.

5. Divide the dough into 6 equal-sized portions.

6. Roll each portion into a ball, then flatten with a rolling pin in between sheets of parchment paper.

7. Refrigerate until ready to use.

8. To cook, heat in a non-stick pan for 2-3 minutes per side.

Prepare the moutabelle:

9. Split each eggplant in half lengthwise. Brush with olive oil and season with salt.

10. Grill over high heat until fully cooked. Set aside until cool enough to handle.

11. Peel the grilled eggplants, and transfer the flesh to a blender or food processor.

12. Add in remaining ingredients and process until smooth. You may add a little warm water if it is too thick to process.

Nutrition: Calories 171 / Carbohydrates 9 g / Fats 15 g / Protein 2 g

Vegetable Latkes Spiked with Curry

Preparation Time: 15 minutes - Cooking Time: 6 min. - Servings: 6

Ingredients:

- 100 grams Carrots, spiralized
- 100 grams Zucchini, spiralized
- 100 grams Cauliflower, minced
- 50 grams minced White Onion
- 5 grams Parsley, chopped
- ¼ cup Almond Flour
- 1 tbsp. Flax Seeds, soaked in 2 tbsp. Water
- 2 tsp Curry Powder - ½ tsp Salt
- 2 tbsp. Olive Oil plus more for frying

Directions:

1. In a bowl, mix almond flour, egg, parsley, onions, curry powder, and salt.
2. In a non-stick skillet over medium heat, heat olive oil.
3. Using a spoon, add vegetable mixture to the hot oil, while you shape every latke like an egg ring.
4. Over medium heat, fry each side for about 3 minutes.
5. Use paper towels to drain.

Nutrition: Calories 123 / Carbohydrates 5 g / Fats 12 g / Protein 2 g

Vegan Cheese Fondue

Preparation Time: 5 minutes - Cooking Time: 20 min. - Servings: 4

Ingredients:

- 70 grams Raw Cashews
- 1 tbsp. Nutritional Yeast
- 1 tsp Garlic Powder
- 2 tsp Cider Vinegar
- 2 tbsp. Gelatin
- 1 tbsp. Turmeric Powder
- 1 tsp Salt - cups Water
- 200 grams Zucchini, cut into sticks

Directions:

1. Boil cashews over high heat in a saucepan for 14 minutes.
2. Blend garlic powder, cashews, gelatin, vinegar, turmeric powder, water, yeast, and salt until smooth.
3. Add the puree to a saucepot and boil for about 4-5 minutes, while constantly stirring. Stir until the mixture is smooth.
4. Put it to a fondue pot and enjoy alongside zucchini sticks.

Nutrition: Calories 126 / Carbohydrates 9 g / Fats 8 g / Protein 6 g

Chocolate Peanut Butter Cookies

Preparation Time: 20 minutes - Cooking Time: 10 min. - Servings: 14

Ingredients:

- ½ cup Peanut Butter, melted
- 3 tbsp. Coconut Oil
- ½ cup Vegan Semi-Sweet Chocolate Chips
- ½ cup Erythritol
- ½ cup Coconut Milk
- 1 tsp Vanilla Extract
- 2 cups Almond Flour
- ½ teaspoon Salt
- ½ teaspoon Baking Soda

Directions:

1. Stir together peanut butter, coconut oil, vanilla extract erythritol, and coconut milk in a bowl.
2. In a separate bowl, whisk together baking soda, flour, and salt.
3. Stir the dry mixture into the wet mixture.
4. Fold the chocolate chips in.
5. Shape dough into cookies and arrange on a baking tray lined with parchment paper. Bake for 10 minutes at 375°F.

Nutrition: Calories 179 / Carbohydrates 5 g / Fats 16 g / Protein 5 g

Veggie Wraps with Glorious Tahini Sauce

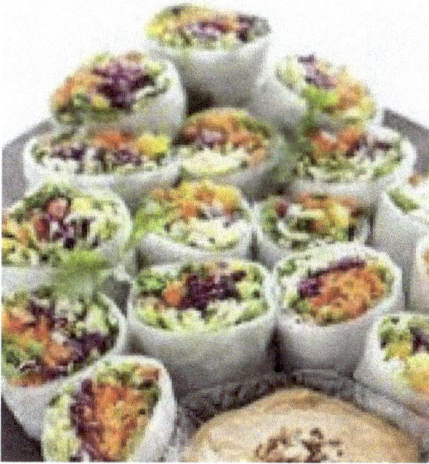

Preparation Time: 10 minutes - Cooking Time: 0 min. - Servings: 8

Ingredients

- ¼ cup of sliced carrots
- 2 tablespoon of sauerkraut
- 2 tablespoon of tahini sauce

Directions

1. De-vein your leaves and wash them well
2. Add carrots, sauerkraut and wrap them up well
3. Pour the sauce directly/use as a dip
4. Enjoy!

Nutrition: Calories: 120 / Fat: 8 g / Carbs: 6 g / Protein: 4 g

Never Fear Thin Bagels Pieces

Preparation Time: 10 minutes

Cooking Time: 40 min.

Servings: 8

Ingredients

- 3 tablespoon of ground flaxseed
- ½ a cup of tahini
- ½ a cup of Psyllium Husk powder
- 1 cup of water
- 1 teaspoon of baking powder
- Just a pinch of salt
- Sesame seeds for garnish

Directions

1. Preheat your oven to 375 degrees Fahrenheit
2. Take a mixing bowl and add Psyllium Husk, baking powder, ground flax seeds, salt and keep whisking until combined
3. Add water to the dry mix and keep mixing until the water has been absorbed fully
4. Add tahini and keep mixing until the dough forms
5. Knead well
6. Form patties from the dough that have a diameter of 4 inches and a thickness of ¼ inch
7. Lay them carefully on your baking tray
8. Cut up a small hole in the middle
9. Add sesame seeds on top
10. Bake for 40 minutes until a golden brown texture is seen
11. Cut them in half and toast if you like
12. Top them up with your favorite Keto-Vegan compliant spread
13. Enjoy!

Nutrition: Calories: 129 / Fat: 10 g / Carbs: 2 g / Protein: 4 g

Very White Chocolate Peanut Butter Bites

Preparation Time: 110 minutes - Cooking Time: 0 min. - Servings: 8

Ingredients

- ½ a cup of cacao butter
- ½ a cup of salted peanut butter
- 3 tablespoon of Stevia
- 4 tablespoon of powdered coconut milk
- 2 teaspoon of vanilla extract

Directions

1. Set your double boiler on low heat
2. Melt the cacao butter and peanut butter together and stir in vanilla extract
3. Take another bowl and add powdered coconut powder and Stevia
4. Stir one tablespoon at a time of the mixture into the vanilla extract mixture
5. Portion the mixture into silicone molds or lined up muffin tins and chill them for 90 minutes
6. Remove and enjoy it!

Nutrition: Calories: 77 / Fat: 7g / Carbs: 8g / Protein: 2g

DESSERTS

Wonderful Peanut Butter Mousse

Preparation Time: 2 to 5 minutes

Cooking Time: 0 minutes - Servings: 4

Ingredients:

- 4 tablespoons natural unsweetened peanut butter
- ½ can coconut cream
- 1 ½ teaspoons stevia

Directions:

1. First of all, please check that you've all the ingredients obtainable. Now combine all ingredients & whip for one minute, until mixture forms peaks.

2. Finally, chill for at least three hours or until a mousse texture is achieved.

Nutrition:Calories: 206 / Protein: 5 g / Fat: 18 g / Carbs: 6 g

The No-Bake Keto Cheese Cake

Preparation Time: 120 minutes

Cooking Time: 0 min.

Servings: 4

Ingredients

For Crust

- 2 tablespoon of ground flaxseed
- 2 tablespoon of desiccated coconut
- 1 teaspoon of cinnamon

For Filling

- 4 ounce of vegan cream cheese
- 1 cup of soaked cashews
- ½ a cup of frozen blueberries
- 2 tablespoon of coconut oil
- 1 tablespoon of lemon juice
- 1 teaspoon of vanilla extract
- Liquid Stevia

Directions

1. Take a container and mix all of the crust ingredients
2. Mix them well and flatten them at the bottom to prepare the crust
3. Take a blender and mix all of the filling ingredients and blend until smooth
4. Distribute the filling on top of your coat and chill it in your freezer for about 2 hours
5. Enjoy!

Nutrition: Calories: 182 / Fat: 16 g / Carbs: 6 g / Protein: 3 g

Raspberry Chocolate Cups

Preparation Time: 60 minutes - Cooking Time: 0 min. - Servings: 12

Ingredients

- ½ a cup of cacao butter
- ½ a cup of coconut manna
- 4 tablespoon of powdered coconut milk
- 3 tablespoon of granulated sugar substitute
- 1 teaspoon of vanilla extract
- ¼ cup of dried and crushed frozen raspberries

Directions

1. Melt cacao butter and add coconut manna
2. Stir in vanilla extract
3. Take another dish and add coconut powder and sugar substitute
4. Stir the coconut mix into the cacao butter, 1 tablespoon at a time, making sure to keep mixing after each addition
5. Add the crushed dried raspberries
6. Mix well and portion it out into muffin tins
7. Chill for 60 minutes and enjoy it!

Nutrition: Calories: 158 / Fat: 15 g / Carbs: 1 g / Protein: 3 g

Awesome Roasted Acorn Squash

Preparation Time: 40 to 45 minutes

Cooking Time: 0 minutes - Servings: 4

Ingredients:

- ¼ teaspoon black pepper
- ¼ cup parmesan cheese, grated
- 8 fresh thyme sprigs
- 2 ½ tablespoons olive oil
- 1 large acorn squash, cut in half lengthwise

Directions:

1. First of all, please certify you've all the ingredients on the market. Preheat the oven to 4000 F. /2000 C.
2. Now remove the seed from squash & cut into ¾ slices.
3. Add squash slices, parmesan cheese, olive oil, thyme, pepper, and salt in a bowl and toss to coat.
4. One thing remains to be done. Then spread squash onto a baking tray & roast in preheated oven for about 25 to 30 minutes or until golden brown.
5. Finally, serve & enjoy.

Nutrition: Calories: 253 / Protein: 12.9 g / Fat: 16.1 g / Carbs: 11.3 g

Exuberant Pumpkin Fudge

Preparation Time: 120 minutes

Cooking Time: 0 min.

Servings: 25

Ingredients

- 1 and a ¾ cup of coconut butter
- 1 cup of pumpkin puree
- 1 teaspoon of ground cinnamon
- ¼ teaspoon of ground nutmeg
- 1 tablespoon of coconut oil

Directions

1. Take an 8x8 inch square baking pan and line it with aluminum foil to start with

2. Take a spoon of the coconut butter and add into a heated pan; let the butter melt over low heat

3. Toss in the spices and pumpkin and keep stirring it until a grainy texture has formed

4. Pour in the coconut oil and keep stirring it vigorously in order to make sure that everything is combined nicely

5. Scoop up the mixture into the previously prepared baking pan and distribute evenly

6. Place a piece of wax paper over the top of the mixture and press on the upper side to make evenly straighten up the topside

7. Remove the wax paper and throw it away

8. Place the mixture in your fridge and let it cool for about 1-2 hours

9. Take it out and cut it into slices, then eat

Nutrition: Calories: 120 / Protein: 1.2 g / Carbs: 4.2 g / Fats: 10.7 g

Lucky Mediterranean Style Pasta

Preparation Time: 10 to 15 minutes

Cooking Time: 5 minutes

Servings: 4

Ingredients:

- 1 cup Spinach
- Salt and black pepper to taste
- 2 ½ tablespoons Olive oil
- 2 tablespoons Butter
- 5 cloves Garlic (minced)
- ¼ cup Feta cheese (crumbled)
- ¼ cup Sun-dried tomatoes
- 2 tablespoons capers
- ¼ cup Parmesan cheese(shredded)
- 2 tablespoons Italian flat-leaf parsley(chopped)
- 10 Kalamata olives(halved)
- 2 Zucchini(spiralized)

Directions:

1. First of all, please confirm you've all the ingredients on the market.

2. Now please heat oil and butter in a large pan& sauté the garlic, spinach, zucchini, in its seasoned with salt & pepper until the spinach wilts & zucchini becomes tender

3. Now drain any extra liquid.

4. One thing remains to be done. Now quickly add the rest of the ingredients except the cheese and stir cook properly for about 2 to 5 minutes.

5. Finally, remove from the flame & toss in the cheese.

Nutrition: Calories: 231 / Protein: 6.5 g / Fat: 20 g / Carbs: 6.5 g

Unique Scrambled Tofu

Preparation Time: 5 to 10 minutes

Cooking Time: 0 minutes

Servings: 1

Ingredients:

- Pepper to taste
- 1 ½ tablespoon grapeseed oil
- 1 tablespoon vegetable broth
- ¼ teaspoon garlic powder
- 1 teaspoon nutritional yeast
- 14 ounces soft tofu
- ¾ teaspoon salt
- 1 teaspoon onion powder
- ¼ teaspoon turmeric powder

Directions:

1. First off all go ahead and assemble all the ingredients at one place. In a small bowl, thoroughly combine nutritional yeast, spices, salt, and pepper. Set aside.

2. Now crumble the tofu depending on how "chunky" you want the scramble to be. Set aside.

3. Please heat oil in a pan on moderate.

4. Now we can plow ahead to succeeding the most significant step. Add tofu & stir until heated through.

5. Add vegetable broth and the spice mix.

6. Now stir until the tofu is evenly coated with the spices.

7. Only one thing remains to be done now. Take off the warmth once most of the liquid is absorbed.

8. Finally, serve hot or warm. Finally, we've completed the recipe. Enjoy.

Nutrition: Calories: 256.5 / Protein: 27 g / Fat: 16.2 g / Carbs: 5.3 g

Quick Creamed Coconut Curry Spinach

Preparation Time: 30 to 35minutes

Cooking Time: 5 minutes

Servings: 6

Ingredients:

- 1 small can whole fat coconut milk
- Cashews for garnish
- 2 ½ teaspoons yellow curry paste
- 1 pound frozen spinach, thawed and drained of moisture
- 1 ½ teaspoon lemon zest

Directions:

1. First of all, please certify you've all the ingredients out there. Please heat a medium-sized available. Please heat a medium-sized pan to medium-high heat, then add the curry paste & cook appropriately for about 30 to 40 seconds.

2. Then add a small amount of the coconut milk & stir to combine and then cook until the paste is aromatic.

3. This step is essential. Add the spinach, and then season.

4. Now quickly add the rest of the ingredients, apart from the cashews, & allow the sauce to reduce slightly.

5. One thing remains to be done. Keep the sauce creamy, but reduce it to coat the spinach thoroughly.

6. Finally, serve with chopped cashews.

Nutrition: Calories: 191 / Protein: 4 g / Fat: 18 g / Carbs: 3 g

Vintage Moist Almond Cake

Preparation Time: 1 hour

Cooking Time: 30 minutes

Servings: 8

Ingredients:

- 5 oz. sugar
- 1 cup Greek yogurt, vanilla(full fat)
- 1 cup almond flour
- 1 ½ teaspoons baking powder
- 1 egg
- ¼ teaspoons baking soda
- 1 ½ teaspoons vanilla
- ¼ teaspoons salt
- 2 oz. butter (soft)
- ½ teaspoon cinnamon powder

Directions:

1. First of all, please confirm you've all the ingredients accessible. Grease a 0- inch layer cake tin and sprinkle with a little almond flour. Heat oven to about 3600 F. to 3700 F.

2. Now sift your salt, cinnamon powder, baking soda, baking powder, almond flour, & sugar in a large bowl. Stir to combine, and set aside.

3. This step is essential. Place in a blender, banana, egg, butter, sugar, and vanilla.

4. Then blend for about 2 minutes at super-speed; consistency should be smooth.

5. Pour blended mixture into almond flour mixture & mix thoroughly.

6. One thing remains to be done. Pour and scrape into the greased tin.

7. Finally, place in oven and bake for about 25 to 30 minutes. Cool & serve.

Nutrition: Calories: 157 / Protein: 2.3 g / Fat: 8 g / Carbs: 19.5 g

Iconic Braised Endives

Preparation Time: 20 to 25 minutes

Cooking Time: 35 minutes

Servings: 2

Ingredients:

- 1 ¾ oz. Butter
- Salt and pepper to taste
- 1 tablespoon Lemon juice
- 3 Endives(chopped lengthwise, brown bruised bits discarded)
- 3 ½ tablespoon Water

Directions:

1. First of all, please check that you've all the ingredients out there. Melt the butter in a non-stick place the endives in it.
2. Then season with salt and pepper & sprinkle the lemon juice on top.
3. Now leave to brown for about 5 to 10 minutes and then flip.
4. Finally, add a little water to the pan & cook covered for about 20 to 25 minutes.

Nutrition: Calories: 225 / Protein: 3 g / Fat: 21 g / Carbs: 9 g

CONCLUSION

There is a point at which veganism and the ketogenic diet meet to produce the keto vegan diet. However, this is hard to conceive because, in terms of what dieters are allowed to consume, vegan diets and the ketogenic diet seem to be polar opposites. Obviously, the vegan and keto diets are similar at some point because they both involve excluding certain items from your diet to achieve certain benefits. The disparity comes in when considering the type of foods to be excluded from the diet.

Notwithstanding, combining Keto and Vegan diets yield enormous benefits and is, therefore, a step further for those who want it. One of the very essences of a vegan lifestyle is to lose weight. Vegans adopt different forms of eating habits just to be able to shed some weight and live a healthier life. However, the natural ketogenic diet, which is high in fat and low in carbs, is known to burn ten times more fat than any other regular diet program. As a result of this, anyone on the vegan diet to lose weight is advised to expand their diet horizon.

Studies have shown that it is possible to gain weight while on the vegan diet since their focus on fruits and vegetables tends to be more carb-heavy and fat-deficient than other diets. Consequently, if the vegan diet is not helping you get that appropriate weight loss, then switching to a keto vegan diet might do the trick.

But how do you combine the vegan and the Keto diet when at their core, both diets contradict each other? The crux of taking up a vegan diet plan is to provide healthful carbohydrates, but keto diets are very low in carbs. Invariably, depending on how strictly you follow the vegan diet, you would probably stay away from meat, fish, and other forms of protein. The question here is how you, as a vegan, add this seemingly complex ketogenic diet, bearing in mind that it contains protein. Trying to think of a way of balancing the two can be mind-boggling. However, one way of effectively combining these two diets will be adding lots of low-carb veggies, as well as dairy. You can also cycle in and out of Ketosis as a way of successfully combining your vegan and Keto diets. Initially, the Keto diet was not meant to be for a long-term basis, so it is possible to combine both.

Also, you will need to focus on whole foods, which, according to Sharon Palmer, helps you maintain energy levels longer. Vegans following the Keto diet stand the risk of being deficient in certain nutrients, vitamins, and minerals, so it would be very wise to seek the counsel of registered dietitian nutritionists to ensure you meet your needs. As a beginner, you need a lot of pointers in relation to the keto vegan lifestyle. The combination of both diets needs proper supervision and understanding to give you the right results. The wrong implementation of the keto vegan diet can cause serious complications, so try to find out the necessary things to start up this diet.

There are some notable benefits you stand to enjoy when on a keto vegan diet, although having the right techniques and strategies will help you get the following benefits from this relatively complicated eating plan.

Combining the vegan and ketogenic diet helps you burn fat a lot faster until you have reached a healthy weight. By adopting the low carb-high fat diet, you are able to lose those fats, including that stubborn belly fat, rapidly. Even without intense exercises, you surely can still see some evidence of weight loss when on the keto vegan diet.

Furthermore, going on the right keto vegan diet provides you with more energy. When you are on a carb-heavy diet, your body is continuously going through a cycle of converting carbs into glucose, thereby elevating your blood sugar levels. There will be energy spikes as a result of this process which may later leave you hungry and depleted, but adding the Keto diet into the mix will help you regulate your cravings. By burning fat steadily for a long time, your system has more consistent levels of energy, thereby reducing the cravings for food.

Not only does the keto vegan diet help you to lose weight, but it also prevents a host of neurodegenerative disorders. These include Alzheimer's disease, Parkinson's disease, and sleep disorders. By intently following the keto vegan diet, you properly nourish and protect the brain. As a matter of fact, Ketogenic diets have also been proven to reduce the risk of developing cardiac diseases, including high triglycerides, hypertension, and LDL cholesterol.

9 781914 029851